A RING OF FIERY HORSES

2 Kings 2:1-14; 6:8-23 FOR CHILDREN

Written by Mervin Marquardt

Illustrated by Vaccaro Associates

ARCH Books

Copyright © 1973 by Concordia Publishing House, St. Louis, Missouri

Concordia Publishing House Ltd., London, E. C. 1

Manufactured in the United States of America

All Rights Reserved

ISBN 0-570-06074-5

Gehazi slowly walked the sand;
his feet could go no faster.
He wished that something soon would show
what happened to his master.

He looked behind some rocks and said,
"He must be someplace near.
My master and his teacher too,
they can't just disappear."

"Elisha! Master!" loud he called.
"Elijah! Teacher! Hear me!
Where are you both? Please answer me!
Why wouldn't you stay near me?"

Then suddenly Gehazi saw
Elisha nearby walking
and carrying Elijah's coat.
Gehazi started talking.

"O Master, I'm so thankful you
are safe from every creature!
But tell me where Elijah is;
we must protect your teacher."

Elisha said, "He's gone away;
God's horses, six or seven,
came flying with a chariot
and took him up to heaven.

"Now quickly we must hurry home,
before we've even rested,
and tell them all God's strength in me
comes with this coat; God blessed it."

They picked an easy path back home
except it crossed a river.
Gehazi planned to swim across,
though water made him shiver.

Elisha knew just what to do,
he never hesitated.
He hit the river with the coat,
and the water separated.

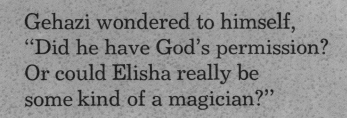

Gehazi wondered to himself,
"Did he have God's permission?
Or could Elisha really be
some kind of a magician?"

For many years Gehazi heard
Elisha's words; but mostly
he followed where Elisha went
and watched his actions closely.

He sweetened water tasting bad
to men and even cattle.
He also helped his country and
his king to win a battle.

Elisha raised the dead to life
(when nobody was looking).
And once he took the poison from
a pot of food while cooking.

And when Gehazi saw all this,
he said, "I know it's true
that God is with Elisha—but
does God protect me too?"

Then one time some years later on
an evil king came riding
to capture old Elisha, who
in Dothan town was hiding.

The king commanded, most unkind,
"Surround the town of Dothan!
Elisha and Gehazi find!
And when you do, kill both, man!"

Gehazi counted the soldiers there
as best as he was able,
then ran to tell Elisha, who
sat calmly at a table.

"O Master, what can we do now?
A thousand men with spears
are marching here to kill us both,"
Gehazi said with tears.

"Relax, my friend," Elisha said,
"and do not be afraid.
For God is here and stronger than
this army men have made."

Elisha knelt and prayed, "O Lord,
Please show my friend so frightened
the things that I already see."
Just then the skies were brightened.

And suddenly Gehazi saw
a ring of fiery horses
and chariots which God had sent,
a host of heavenly forces.

Then finally Gehazi said,
"I won't forget this ever.
I know that God protects me and
will keep me safe forever."

Dear Parents:

This Arch book story of the prophet Elisha is based on 2 Kings 2:1-14 and 6:8-23. It is written from the standpoint of Elisha's servant, Gehazi, a man who faced the same doubt many of us face.

Elisha's teacher was the great prophet Elijah. Elisha received twice as much of God's Spirit as Elijah; yet Elijah's popularity may have overshadowed Elisha. Some may have wondered (as Gehazi does in this book) if Elisha was even sent by God. This is suggested by what happened after Elijah was taken up to heaven. Fifty men spent three days in the desert looking for his body. Perhaps they thought Elisha had killed him.

Gehazi, at least, could doubt no longer when at one point God opened his eyes. Gehazi saw the heavenly hosts protecting Elisha.

As with Gehazi, many people would like a special sign or revelation from God. All of us, including our children, need to remember the point of this story: God's protective love exists whether anyone sees it or not.

After sharing this story with your child, discuss any times he would have liked to see a special sign from God, or times he wondered if God *really* loved or protected him. We do have a clear and certain sign from God: our Lord Jesus. God Himself became man, lived, died, and came back to life again, so that everyone could see in his heart what Gehazi saw with his eyes.

The Editor